THE REPLAY

Written by

Adam Skinner

Illustrated by

Mai Ly Degnan

MAGIC CAT 🐱 PUBLISHING

NEW YORK

For my mum, Kim, who was taken too soon,
and Hannah, who lights up the room -A.S.

For my husband, Matthew; my agent Sylvie;
and my dear pug, Uncle Fester -M.L.D.

The illustrations were created in pencil and colored digitally
Set in Citrus Gothic, Krub, Mathlete, Nordic Club, and Patrick Hand.

Library of Congress Control Number 2021951419
ISBN 978-1-4197-6023-5

Text © 2022 Magic Cat Publishing
Illustrations © 2022 Mai Ly Degnan
Book design by Nicola Price
Cover © 2022 Magic Cat

Printed and bound in China
10 9 8 7 6 5 4 3 2 1

Abrams Books are available at special discounts when purchased in quantity for premiums and promotions
as well as fundraising or educational use. Special editions can also be created to specification. For details, contact
specialsales@abramsbooks.com or the address below.

ABRAMS The Art of Books
195 Broadway, New York, NY 10007
abramsbooks.com

SOMETIMES, SPORTS SERVE UP MOMENTS SO SPECIAL THEY LIVE ON FOREVER.

It can take a single kick of a ball to bring a nation together, or two powerful raised fists to change the course of history. As records are smashed and hardships are overcome, sports inspire us to be our best selves as we witness our favorite athletes achieving feats we can't even begin to comprehend.

Get ready to take a front-row seat and relive some of these incredible moments. We have broken each one down, frame by frame, so you can experience the pressure of taking a penalty in front of one hundred thousand fans like Brandi Chastain and fly through the air with Michael Jordan. You'll chip from the rough with Tiger Woods and your head will spin performing the 1080 twist of Kelly Clark. We'll take you to the heart of Africa, the sweeping Italian countryside, and some awe-inspiring Olympic stadiums where you'll witness incredible displays of individual brilliance, gutsy teamwork, and shocking upsets that nobody could have predicted.

This book is a celebration of sports and a reminder that all great athletes started where you are now. No matter your age, size, or skill, there is a sport for you . . . and who knows, maybe one day you will create a great sports moment of your own.

CONTENTS

MICHAEL JORDAN'S
FOUL-LINE DUNK

Have you ever dreamed of having the power to fly? Well, you don't have to be a superhero, as Michael Jordan proved when he defied the laws of gravity to produce the most amazing dunk ever seen.

I t was 1988, and the world's greatest basketball player was ready for takeoff at the annual NBA Slam Dunk Contest.

Chicago Bulls star Jordan and Atlanta Hawks rival Dominique Wilkins had cruised to the final by wowing the judges. With three dunks each to be scored out of a possible 50 points, Wilkins gained an early lead. Jordan would need to score at least 49 on his final dunk to win. Performing any dunk is never easy, but Jordan had to produce something truly spectacular. And boy did he deliver.

BIG HANG THEORY

"Hang time" is the amount of time a person can remain in the air after leaving the ground. Jordan became widely known as "His Airness" due to the incredible amount of hang time he was able to achieve. The average hang time is around half a second. Jordan achieved the extraordinary as he stayed airborne for a mind-blowing 0.92 seconds!

Silence falls over the crowd as they hold their breath. Jordan focuses in on the hoop.

The crowd roars to life as Jordan sets off with the ball in hand.

Picking up speed, he dribbles past the crowd of photographers capturing the moment on film . . .

and keeps his cool as he approaches the foul line.

He plants his foot and, with the ball in one hand . . .

launches himself upward.

Up, up, up!

He treads the air like water.

Is it a bird? Is it a plane? No, it's Michael Jordan soaring through the air!

Wahhhowee!

He slams the ball home to score a **perfect 50** from the judges . . .

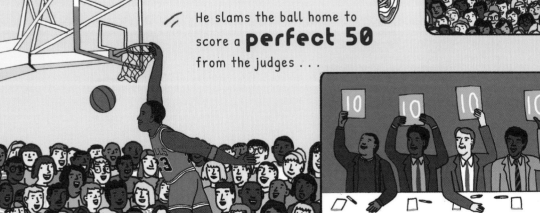

and wins the 1988 NBA Slam Dunk Contest!

BETHANY HAMILTON

PLACES FIRST AT SURF N SEA PIPELINE PRO

Bethany Hamilton was born to surf. At thirteen years old, her dream of turning professional appeared to be over when she lost her arm in a shark attack. But Hamilton was determined to get back into the water, returning to her board just days after the attack.

Hamilton's unrivaled courage led to her first national surfing title within two years of her attack, and she claimed the ESPY Award for Best Comeback Athlete in 2004.

But it was on a balmy March day in Hawaii, eleven years after the shark attack, when the resilient Hamilton won the Surf N Sea Pipeline Women's Pro, a major event in women's surfing. Pitted against the best surfers on the planet, Hamilton won every single heat as she threw some giant turns into the waves before finishing off with a stunning backhand snap to claim victory.

Hamilton begins her run. The Hawaiian native knows these waters—she attacks the incoming wave and throws a quality turn.

Smooth as you like, Hamilton touches down and glides across the water.

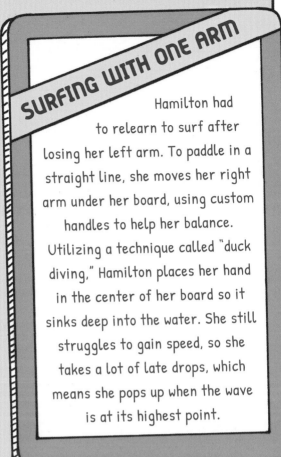

SURFING WITH ONE ARM

Hamilton had to relearn to surf after losing her left arm. To paddle in a straight line, she moves her right arm under her board, using custom handles to help her balance. Utilizing a technique called "duck diving," Hamilton places her hand in the center of her board so it sinks deep into the water. She still struggles to gain speed, so she takes a lot of late drops, which means she pops up when the wave is at its highest point.

The wave is getting bigger now, but Hamilton is not about to be put off by a six-footer.

She throws an impressive right-foot turn . . .

pulling the move off to **perfection!**

Eyes fixed on the final wave, Hamilton begins her ascent.

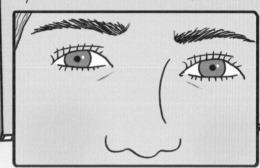

In the blink of an eye she hits the crest of the wave and spins.

She just needs to stay on her feet for a moment longer . . .

WHOOSH! Hamilton caresses the water on the way back down, and the waves roar behind her as she secures her victory!

Returning to shore, Hamilton receives a hero's welcome . . .

and is officially crowned champion of the Surf N Sea Pipeline Women's Pro!

MUHAMMAD ALI WINS THE RUMBLE IN THE JUNGLE

Muhammad Ali proclaimed himself "the Greatest"—and it is hard to disagree. Outside the ring, he won people's hearts and minds by fighting for equality and racial justice. Inside, he won some of the most iconic fights that boxing has ever seen.

Moonlight shone down on the outdoor 20th of May Stadium in 1974 as sixty thousand spectators gathered to watch Africa's first heavyweight championship match.

Current undefeated heavyweight champion "Big George" Foreman and rival Ali, the former heavyweight champion, spent much of the year training in Zaire (now the Democratic Republic of the Congo) getting acclimated to its tropical climate before their match there. In temperatures around 80 degrees, Foreman felt confident: He was young, undefeated, and had recently knocked out the two men who had beaten Ali. Although Ali might be past his prime, the former champ was ready. He knew he couldn't match Foreman for muscle. Instead, he'd have to outsmart him.

Ding!

The sound of the opening bell rings through the stadium. Ali and Foreman clench their fists and lift up their gloves.

The crowd erupts as Ali strikes first, but then Foreman unleashes a mighty blow!

MUHAM ALI

Ali backs into the ropes, countering Foreman's punches with small, but forceful, jabs.

Foreman delivers strike after strike over seven brutal rounds, but into the eighth, he begins to tire.

Ali takes this opportunity and peels himself off the ropes.

He lunges forward and delivers a huge right-hand blow . . .

Whack!

Foreman is sent tumbling toward the canvas!

Standing over the fallen giant, Ali hears the crowd chanting his name:

Ali! **Ali!** **Ali!**

The referee starts to count, **"One, two, three . . ."** Foreman unsuccessfully tries to gather his strength and rise. **". . . eight, nine, ten."**

"Knockout!"

Muhammad Ali is the new heavyweight champion of the world!

ROPE-A-DOPE

Foreman was considered the favorite to win due to his superior punching power, so in an attempt to avoid many of his heaviest blows, Ali chose to fight leaning back into the ropes. This was Ali's classic "rope-a-dope" strategy. It allowed much of the punch's energy to be absorbed by the ropes' elasticity rather than Ali's body, while still tiring Foreman out.

USAIN BOLT
SMASHES THE 100-METER WORLD RECORD

From 2008 to 2009, Usain Bolt crushed the men's 100-meter world record three times. By running it in a mind-blowing time of 9.58 seconds at the World Championships in Germany, the Jamaican sprint king cemented his place as the fastest person in the history of planet Earth.

At the age of just twenty-two, on a Berlin night in August 2009, Bolt produced his greatest ever performance on the track . . .

He had stormed to Olympic gold in a world-record time of 9.69 seconds a year earlier, but now the world title was in his sights. Standing in his way was a field of superstar athletes that included defending champion Tyson Gay. It was billed as a showdown between Bolt and his American rival that promised to be a tense battle. But what happened next was something quite different. With his enormous strides and blistering speed, Bolt blows past Gay and the rest of the chasing pack, leaving them trailing in his dust on the way to a record that stands to this day.

"Are you ready? I'm ready!"
Bolt says to his fans watching at home.

THE WORLD'S FASTEST HUMAN
At this record-winning event, Bolt's average ground speed was an incredible 23.35 miles per hour. Even more astounding is that Bolt started from a speed of zero and then had to accelerate, which means that his top speed was 27.78 miles per hour—quicker than a charging elephant!

ON YOUR MARKS . . . Bolt takes center stage in lane four. He places his feet on the blocks.

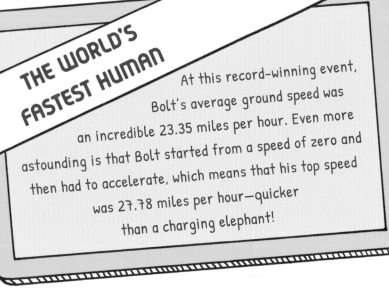

GET SET . . .

He places his head down, back toward the sky.

GO!

The starting pistol is heard across the stadium as a roar echoes from the crowd.

Bolt and Gay explode out of the blocks. It's the perfect start for both of them—this could be close.

But Bolt takes it up a notch.

Blink and you'll miss him—Bolt's arms pump at a lightning speed! With his enormous strides and explosive acceleration, Bolt races past Gay.

He crosses the finish line a massive **TWO METERS** ahead of the chasing pack!

Bolt knows he was quick. He checks the clock: **9.58 seconds**—a new world record!

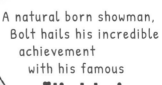

A natural born showman, Bolt hails his incredible achievement with his famous "lightning bolt" celebration.

TORVILL AND DEAN
ACHIEVE A PERFECT SCORE

Some say perfection is not possible. But try telling that to British ice dancers Jayne Torvill and Christopher Dean, who achieved just that at the 1984 Winter Olympics in the Bosnian capital, Sarajevo. Their stunning performance not only sealed the illustrious gold medal, but also earned the British stars a perfect score of six for artistic impression from all of the judges.

As reigning world and European champions, Torvill and Dean were already the favorites to win gold before the Olympic Games.

The ice was their natural habitat, after all, but nobody was prepared for the stunning display they were about to witness. The pair took a risk with a tricky interpretation of *Boléro*, an orchestral piece by Maurice Ravel, and the world held its breath in the hope that neither would slip up. There was no need to worry, though, as on the evening of Valentine's Day, the dynamic duo produced a blade-perfect performance full of elegance, passion, and drama that cemented their place as the greatest dancers to have ever graced the ice.

A CLEVER PLAN

Ravel's *Boléro* was originally eighteen minutes long, but Olympic rules said dances could only be four minutes long (plus or minus ten seconds). *Boléro* could be shortened to four minutes, twenty-eight seconds, but this was still too long, so Torvill and Dean needed to come up with a clever plan. Since the timer didn't begin until they actually started skating, they spent the first eighteen seconds dancing on their knees without their skates touching the ice.

To the sound of *Boléro*, Torvill and Dean drop to their knees on the ice.

They gaze into each other's eyes.

Their hands rise and fall, performing sweeping arm gestures that mirror each other flawlessly.

After eighteen tense seconds,

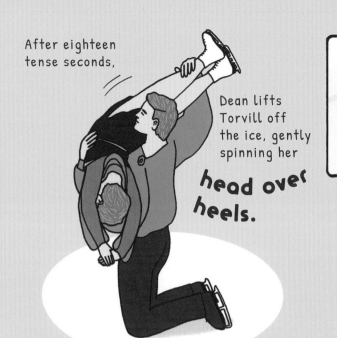

Dean lifts Torvill off the ice, gently spinning her

head over heels.

Torvill's skate caresses the ice for the first time.

WHOOSH!

They glide around the rink in perfect harmony.

It may be cold on the ice, but Torvill and Dean turn up the heat with a sensational lift. It's a risky move . . .

Torvill is entirely carried by Dean's leg while they glide across the ice!

As the music builds, Dean takes the cue to lift his partner up.

Torvill twirls through the air

and lands with her customary grace.

19. TORVILL J.
DEAN C.   GBR
04:04
1   2   3   4   5   6   7   8   9
60 60 60 60 60 60 60 60 60

Dean carries Torvill for one final lift, knowing one false move would see her crash into the ice—but he holds strong—and there's no mistake about it, the gold medal is theirs!

The music comes to a dramatic end and the pair collapse. As they raise their heads from the ice, their eyes turn to the board.

Every judge has awarded a perfect six!

MICHAEL PHELPS
BREAKS A 2,168-YEAR-OLD RECORD

Records are there to be broken. The very best might last for a decade, but most are broken within a few years or months. One particular record, though, had stood since 152 BCE. That was until Michael Phelps came along more than two thousand years later . . .

Phelps sent records tumbling throughout his glittering career.

By the time he arrived in Brazil for the Rio Olympics in 2016, you had to travel back a long time to find a record he hadn't broken. The most decorated Olympian of all time had racked up a whopping eleven golds in individual events, but one man boasted even more: Leonidas of Rhodes. Leonidas was a famous ancient Olympian who won twelve golds at the Olympic Games between 164 and 152 BCE—2,168 years before Phelps entered the pool in Brazil. Phelps tied Leonidas's twelve golds in the 200-meter butterfly and, hours later, achieved victory in the 200-meter individual medley. Phelps claimed his thirteenth individual gold and beat the record for the most golds held by any individual athlete. Amazing!

PEEP, PEEP, PEEP, PEEP! The swimmers take their positions, with Phelps in lane four.

Phelps oozes calm as he enters the arena at the Olympic Aquatics Stadium.

BEEP! The buzzer goes off and the entire field explodes from the blocks.

The swimmers hit the water in unison.

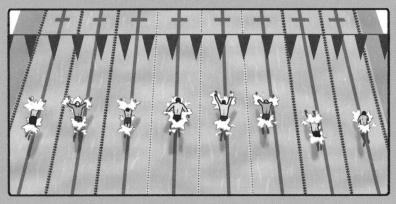

They scramble for position at the start of the butterfly leg and it's neck and neck at the front of the pack.

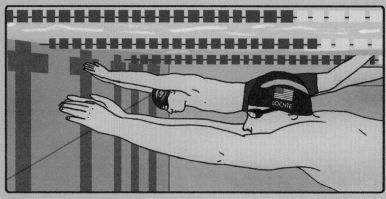

Phelps and fellow American Ryan Lochte cannot be split as they make the first turn.

Phelps propels himself off the side of the pool and powers into the backstroke, but it's Brazilian Thiago Pereira who has taken the lead before his home crowd.

Phelps hits back with every stroke, sweeping his arms over his head while powerfully kicking his legs to edge ahead of Pereira.

MEDAL DETECTOR

After his performance at the 2016 Olympics, Phelps had twenty-three career golds, which was more than many entire countries. In fact, if Phelps himself were a country, he would have been thirty-eighth on the all-time Olympics gold medal table. He had more Olympic gold medals than India, a country with a population of more than 1.3 billion!

Phelps establishes a decent lead as the pack heads into the breaststroke after the third turn.

One turn to go and Phelps is out in front. If he gets this right, then the gold is surely his . . .

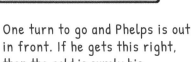

and it's a perfect turn! Phelps storms ahead in the freestyle leg.

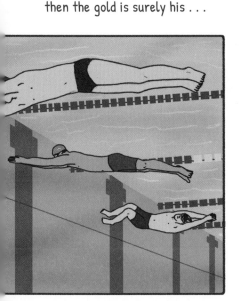

The pack trails in his wake as he takes the gold!

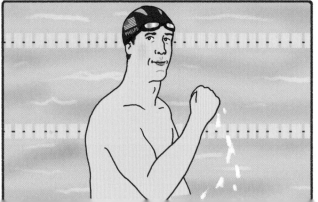

The greatest swimmer of all time catches his breath as the achievement sinks in—he's won **thirteen individual golds!**

JOE MONTANA'S
TOUCHDOWN PASS TO DWIGHT CLARK

How many great catches have been made in NFL history? Hundreds? Thousands? Mention "The Catch," though, and fans will think of only one: Joe Montana to Dwight Clark in the playoffs following the 1981 NFL season.

On January 10, 1982, the Dallas Cowboys reigned as "America's Team," and the San Francisco 49ers were fighting to reach their first Super Bowl.

Needing a touchdown with less than a minute to go, the 49ers found themselves six yards from goal. They decided to run the "Change Left Slot—Sprint Right Option," a play developed by coach Bill Walsh. It almost never worked in practice, but it had to now. After the snap, Montana rolled right, lofted the ball up—and it looked to be heading out of bounds. But Clark leapt, plucked the ball out of the sky with his fingertips, briefly lost control, regained it . . . Touchdown! Ray Wersching kicked the extra point to send the 49ers to the Super Bowl, which they won to start a dynasty that lasted more than a decade.

SPRINT RIGHT OPTION

Head coach Bill Walsh's decision may have made history—but it didn't work out the way he intended. The move was supposed to set up a quick pass to Freddie Solomon, but he slipped and the Cowboys defense was able to chase Montana all the way to the sidelines. To avoid being sacked, Montana launched the ball high into the air. Many believe it was so high, he intended to throw it out. But Montana knew exactly where Clark would be as he ran down the back boundary of the end zone.

It's now or never for the San Francisco 49ers, who trail 21–27. They are one touchdown away from their first ever appearance at the Super Bowl.

Quarterback Montana takes the snap. **SMASH!** The offensive line in front of him looks to take out the Dallas Cowboys's defense . . .

but the offensive line collapses, Montana is backpedaling! Three defenders are in hot pursuit!

His eyes dart around the field looking for his teammate.

He pulls his right arm back, ready to throw—but he'll have to be quick to avoid being sacked!

Hopping onto his right foot, Montana springs from the field and propels his arm forward.

WHOOSH!

The ball is tossed high into the air, threading perfectly between the onrushing defenders.

It heads to the far side of the end zone. The receiver, Clark, reverses his run and sprints down the back boundary.

He jumps up, flying through the air.

Somehow, he clutches the ball in his fingertips!

TOUCHDOWN!

Clark just needs to hold on to score.

The 49ers are going to the Super Bowl!

BILLIE JEAN KING
TRIUMPHS IN THE BATTLE OF THE SEXES

An advocate for gender equality for women from a young age, Billie Jean King accepted a challenge to play a tennis match against former number one-ranked player Bobby Riggs. Her incredible work paved the way for the equal prize money that is in place today.

The odds were stacked against King before her famous clash with Riggs.

Earlier that year, fifty-five-year-old Riggs had beaten the top-ranked women's player, Margaret Court. He boasted of a one-sided contest, and he was right. Just not in the way he thought. At twenty-nine years old, King was fitter, stronger and technically far superior. Promoters named it the "Battle of the Sexes," and thirty thousand fans at the Houston Astrodome in Texas watched King storm to a straight-sets victory in a match that changed the lives of women in the sport.

EQUAL PRIZE MONEY

In the 1960s and 1970s, the tournament pay-outs for female tennis players were significantly lower than those received by male players. In 1973, King lobbied for equal prize money at the US Open by threatening to boycott the tournament. It was introduced shortly before her match with Riggs and, thanks to King's efforts, all four tennis Grand Slams (the Australian Open, French Open, Wimbledon, and the US Open) now pay out equal prize money to male and female players.

Queen of the Court, King receives the royal treatment as she is carried in on a throne.

Riggs is not one to be upstaged—the showman waves to the crowd as he's carried in on a rickshaw.

Relaxed Riggs refuses to take his jacket off—but King won't be distracted as she prepares to serve. The racket comes over her head . . .

SMACK!

The match begins! King swoops through the air to bat a volleyed winner beyond Riggs and takes the opening game.

King	1
Riggs	0

It's Riggs's serve. He lobs the ball up, but King hits a stunning overhead smash to win the first set.

King	6
Riggs	4

The second set is in King's sights as she unleashes a vicious serve—it's too hot to handle and Riggs returns into the net!

King	6	6
Riggs	4	3

Riggs takes his jacket off as a deft volley in the third set sends him running.

He attempts a lob from the back of the court,

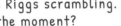

but the ball flies up, up, and . . .

OUT!

King	6	6	5
Riggs	4	3	3

It's match point. Riggs serves and King hits a great forehand return.

It sends Riggs scrambling. Is this the moment?

Yes! Riggs crashes a volley into the net! King hurls her racket into the air to celebrate a **straight-sets victory.**

King	6	6	6
Riggs	4	3	3

TIGER WOODS
SINKS AN "IMPOSSIBLE" CHIP

Tiger Woods's chip on the final day of the 2005 Masters might be the greatest shot in the history of golf. Without even being able to see the hole, he appeared to defy the laws of physics.

When Woods teed off into the rough on the sixteenth hole, his one-shot advantage at the top of the leaderboard was starting to look very slender.

But a true golfing legend was not about to let an impossible shot get between him and glory. He picked a spot twenty-five feet from the hole, and when his ball landed, it took a sharp right turn and sloped toward the hole. The ball eventually crept up to the lip of the cup, where time appeared to freeze. It felt like ages as his ball sat there. After two long, painful seconds, gravity took over. The ball dropped—as did the jaws of everybody watching!

Opting for an eight-iron off the tee at the sixteenth hole, Woods pulls his club back and swings it forward.

WHACK!

His ball appears to be sailing long and wide, landing in the second cut of the rough.

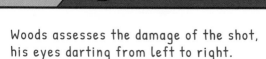

Woods assesses the damage of the shot, his eyes darting from left to right.

Woods needs to compose himself. He bows his head, fixes his eyes on the ball, and lifts a delicate chip onto the green.

The ball skims across the green, landing around twenty-five feet from the hole.

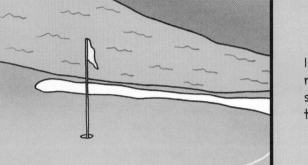

It takes a sharp right turn and slopes its way toward the hole.

Here it comes, creeping ever closer to the cup.

Closer still.

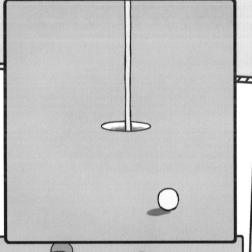

(NOT SO) SWEET SIXTEEN

The Masters is held over four days each year in Augusta, Georgia, and the green at the sixteenth hole is famously unforgiving. This is especially true on the final day as the flag is normally positioned on the left-hand side. The green slopes right to left, and golfers often fly past the hole by over-hitting their approach. But Woods used the slope to his advantage, picking the perfect spot for his ball to land before turning toward the hole and disappearing down it!

Woods watches on, willing his ball into the hole.

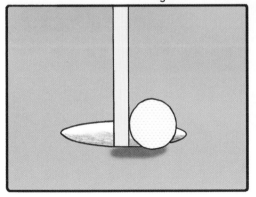

But it stops dead right on the lip—and time appears to stand still . . .

PLOP!

before it somehow drops into the hole!

Woods punches the air in celebration—a spectacular shot from **the best golfer the world has ever seen!**

ANNA VAN DER BREGGEN'S
SOLO ATTACK AT IMOLA

When Anna van der Breggen set off at the 2020 Road World Championships in Imola, Italy, there were 144 other cyclists standing between her and glory. So with twenty-five miles to go, she launched an attack that left a star-studded peloton trailing in her wake.

With the Italian sun shining down on the famous Autodromo Enzo e Dino Ferrari racetrack, a group of nine riders established an early lead during the first of five laps.

Each of them appeared to have a decent shot at victory—but everything changed at the beginning of lap four. As they reached the brutal Cima Gallisterna climb, van der Breggen found strength none of the others could muster. Powering up the hill, she flew past one rider . . . and then another . . . and before the end of the steep slope, the Dutchwoman had broken away from the entire pack—and they didn't see her again for the rest of the race!

And they're off! Van der Breggen and the rest of the group begin the epic race.

Two laps in and van der Breggen is biding her time. The leading pack knows what she can do, so they frequently look back to check where she is.

Then fellow Dutchwoman Marianne Vos moves out to the front! She's one of the best riders of all time, so this could be bad news for van der Breggen . . .

QUEEN OF THE HILLS

Van der Breggen excels when it comes to riding in hilly terrain, which is just as well given the ruthless Imola route. The 89-mile race includes over 900 feet of uphill climbing! Incredibly, just two days before, she won gold in the time trial event and became only the second woman to win both races in the same year.

but Vos looks to be tiring on the slope. Van der Breggen sees an opportunity and makes a break for it!

Powering up the infamous Cima Gallisterna climb, her legs pump the pedals.

VROOM! She powers past Vos and into the lead.

Van der Breggen continues to attack the road in front of her to further open a gap between her and Vos.

She looks back, Vos is nowhere to be seen, but now Italian Elisa Longo Borghini is hot on her heels!

Van der Breggen speeds up to create an enormous lead.

The bell signals the final lap.

RING!

Van der Breggen is now in cruise control, flying around one of the final bends.

She bombs downhill with epic speed . . .

In a flash, it's all over! **The Queen of the Hills** raises her hands in the air as she crosses the finish line to toast an amazing victory.

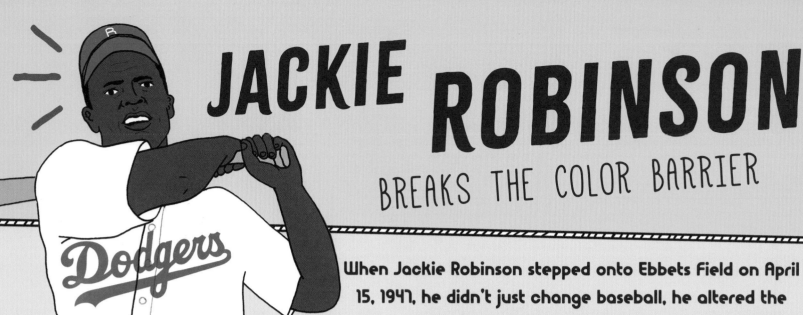

JACKIE ROBINSON

BREAKS THE COLOR BARRIER

When Jackie Robinson stepped onto Ebbets Field on April 15, 1947, he didn't just change baseball, he altered the course of history. Before this momentous day, Black players had been excluded from Major League Baseball and could only play in the so-called "Negro Leagues," where conditions and pay were poor.

In front of a crowd of more than twenty-five thousand spectators in Brooklyn, New York, Robinson became the first Black player of the modern era to play in the major leagues.

When Robinson signed with the Dodgers, racial discrimination in the United States was widespread and often legal. Before the game, some of Robinson's own teammates even threatened to resign over his inclusion and he was subjected to taunts from both fans and opposing players. But that only helped spur him on and it was his incredible play on the field that ultimately silenced them all.

HISTORY MAKERS

By the 1940s, organized baseball had been segregated for more than half a century. Brooklyn Dodgers's manager Branch Rickey decided to change that. After searching for a Black player with the skills and character to handle the pressure of breaking the color barrier, he signed Jackie Robinson to a contract that brought him to the Montreal Royals in 1946. Robinson made his major-league debut with the Dodgers a year later.

Waiting nervously in the dugout, Robinson prepares to make his major-league debut. The Dodgers's newest star rises from the bench . . .

and takes his first step onto the field.

He slowly lifts his head to meet the eye of the Boston Braves's pitcher Johnny Sain.

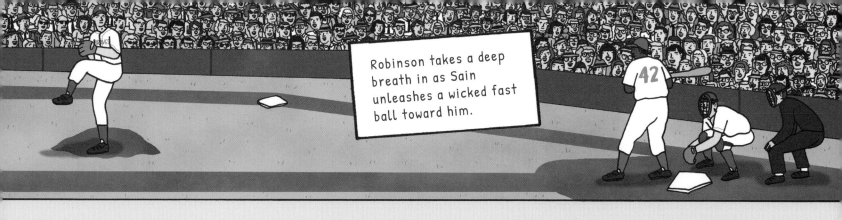

Robinson takes a deep breath in as Sain unleashes a wicked fast ball toward him.

Robinson uses his whole body to swing. **CRACK!** His bat connects with the ball.

Robinson speeds down the baseline, eyes fixed on first base as he goes for a historic first hit . . .

but is denied by a superb piece of fielding by the Braves. So close!

With the Dodgers 3–2 down, Robinson opts to lay down a bunt—and it's a beauty! He sprints to first base.

Bamboozled by Robinson's lightning speed, the Braves make an error.

Robinson gets himself on second.

On the next hit, he takes third . . .

and makes it home!

The crowd erupts as Robinson scores to set up a 5–3 victory. The color barrier has been broken.

Baseball will never be the same again!

CATHY FREEMAN
WINS 400-METER OLYMPIC GOLD

Few people epitomize grace under pressure like sprinter Cathy Freeman at the 2000 Olympics. In her iconic green, white, and yellow bodysuit, the darling of Australian sport became the first Australian Indigenous person to win an individual Olympic gold medal as she powered to victory in the 400-meters.

When Freeman stepped onto the track for the most anticipated final of the Sydney Games, a crowd of more than a hundred thousand nervous spectators held its breath.

The host nation's only hope for athletics gold, Freeman started cautiously behind Jamaica's Lorraine Graham, but picked off the field as the home fans roared her over the line in a speedy 49.11 seconds. "What a legend," commentator Bruce McAveney cried out. "What a champion!"

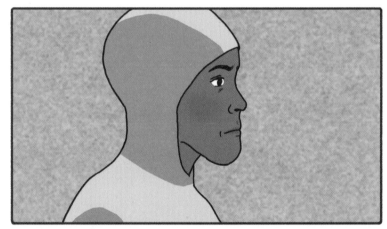

With the weight of a nation on her shoulders, Freeman takes a moment to reflect before taking her marks.

FLYING THE FLAG

After her victory, Freeman flew the Australian and Aboriginal flags on her lap of honor. She had done the same six years earlier and was warned by the head of the Commonwealth Games not to fly the Aboriginal flag again. But Freeman was courageous and, with her shoulders free of the weight of expectation, carried both flags—a symbol of reconciliation and pride in her Aboriginal heritage.

As the starting pistol rings out, she shoots out of the blocks and gets a great start . . .

but so does the rest of the field.

Around the first bend, Freeman appears to be falling back, and Jamaica's Lorraine Graham is lightning quick on the back straight.

Graham continues to hold the lead and with two bends to go, Freeman has a lot of work to do . . .

but here comes Freeman into the final 100 meters, and she's flying!

She has **laser focus**. There's no catching her now . . .

and she crosses the finish line first with meters to spare!

Freeman falls to the ground and cries tears of joy—the homegrown hero is an **Olympic champion!**

This is her moment, she takes a well-deserved victory lap, proudly waving the Australian and Aboriginal flags.

BRANDI CHASTAIN'S
WORLD CUP-WINNING PENALTY

Imagine ninety thousand people watching as you prepare to take a shot. You're 12 yards from the goal. Only the goalkeeper stands between you and victory. A silence falls, the crowd holds its breath, but you can hardly catch your own. Could you hold your nerve? US defender Brandi Chastain did when she stepped up to take a penalty kick in the 1999 World Cup final.

After 120 painful, goalless minutes on a sweltering California summer day, the USA and China faced the lottery of a penalty shootout.

Four perfect penalties from the USA and a miss from China meant Chastain could seal the win by hitting the back of the net. The pressure was immense as she placed the ball on the spot at the Rose Bowl, in front of the biggest crowd to ever watch a women's sporting event. She took six steps back, ran forward, and smashed a left-foot drive into the top corner. Goal! It didn't just win the World Cup, it proved that the women's game could match the men's for excitement and inspired some of the best players in the sport today.

Chastain makes the long, lonely walk to the penalty spot.

A silence falls inside the Rose Bowl as Chastain places the ball.

She retreats—one step, two steps, three steps, four steps, five steps, six.

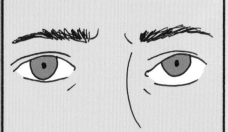

Her teammates look on nervously.

As Chastain turns to face the goal, she takes a breath in.

She runs toward the ball, the balls of her feet pounding the turf.

Chastain smashes the ball to the left, and goalkeeper, Gao Hong, dives for it . . .

but it's just too fast! Chastain's penalty flies high into the top corner . . .

and it nestles into the back of the net!

The silence turns to loud cheers!

FOOT FOR THOUGHT

Chastain was naturally two-footed—a skill very few players can boast. Although she was mainly left-footed in normal play, she mostly took penalties with her right. But for this match, coach Tony DiCicco instructed her to take it with her left, as she had missed a penalty with her right against China just four months earlier. Not only did she strike her penalty kick sweetly, Chastain put it right in the top corner, where experts believe goalkeepers have only a small chance of making a save.

Chastain falls to her knees in celebration.

Team USA is the world champion!

SIMONE BILES

TUMBLES TO TAKE RIO BY STORM

Simone Biles should be celebrated for many reasons. Her extraordinary comeback bronze at the 2020 Tokyo Games after withdrawing to safeguard her mental health was a courageous act, but it was her signature move, "the Biles," which she executed flawlessly at the Rio Games four years earlier, that cemented her place as one of the greatest gymnasts ever.

Biles, who was too young to qualify for the 2012 London Olympics, was a favorite entering the 2016 Games in Rio de Janeiro, Brazil.

She lived up to expectations, first leading the United States to gold in the team event and then winning the individual all-around. To the sound of samba music in the famous Brazilian city, Biles produced a stunning floor routine full of flips, spins, and tumbles that demonstrated her unrivaled power and skill. To cap it off, the American performed "the Biles" to snatch the gold in style, becoming the first female US gymnast to win four gold medals at a single Games!

BILES AHEAD OF THE REST

Performed on the floor exercise, "the Biles" is a double flip with a half twist. The twist comes near the end of the second flip, meaning Biles lands facing forward. (A front landing is much more difficult than a backward landing because gymnasts can't see the ground as they rotate toward it!) The first time Biles tried the move she tore her calf muscle, but at the 2016 Rio Olympics it propelled her to gold in the all-around event.

Dancing to the beat of the samba, the Brazilian crowd is lapping up her routine.

It's all smiles for Biles as she gears up for her floor routine in the all-around event.

But now the show really starts! Biles begins the run up to get the power needed to pull off her signature move.

As her hands touch the floor, Biles twists so she is facing backward—a fantastic roundoff!

The American star quickly flips onto her feet . . .

launching straight into a **back handspring . . .**

which gives her enough power to propel into a **flawless double layout with a half twist!**

She's gone and done it! Biles lands facing forward . . .

and jumps straight into a beautiful stag leap.

What an incredible finish—another **gold medal** is in the bag!

M.S. DHONI

HITS AN ICONIC SIX

When India hosted the ICC World Cup in 2011, the cricket-mad nation had not won the tournament since 1983. Step forward Mahendra Singh Dhoni. With an entire country's hopes resting on his shoulders, team captain Dhoni smashed an epic six against Sri Lanka to bring the trophy home.

Chasing 275 runs—a record for a World Cup final—India had its back to the wall after losing the early wickets of Sachin Tendulkar and Virender Sehwag.

Even when Dhoni came to the crease, the hosts required 161 runs, and the man himself had struggled with the bat all tournament.

But Dhoni put his troubles behind him, smacking 85 runs off the first 78 balls he faced. And when it came to ball 79—in the famous words of commentator Ravi Shastri, he "finished off in style!" Hitting the ball with his bat's sweet spot, he struck an enormous six, sparking celebrations in the Wankhede Stadium and around the entire country.

India has batted their way to the brink of history and it's all down to Dhoni now. He wipes the sweat from his brow and prepares to face the Sri Lankan attack.

Sri Lankan bowler Nuwan Kulasekara thunders down the pitch. His arm rubs his ear and his hand releases the ball.

WHOOSH! It speeds toward captain Dhoni!

As the ball drops and bounces off the pitch, Dhoni gets in line and pulls his bat back and high.

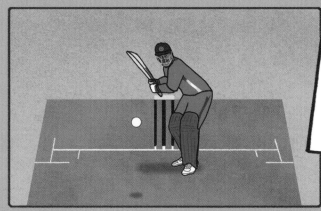

With immense power, he swings the bat forward. **WHACK!** Dhoni connects perfectly with the ball . . .

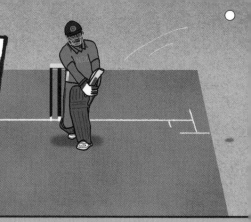

and sends it flying through the air!

The Sri Lanka fielders look on helplessly as the ball flies over their heads.

Up, up, up . . .

Dhoni twirls his bat in the air as he admires his amazing helicopter shot.

A huge roar vibrates across the stands as the ball drops into the crowd—Dhoni has smashed a six!

THE HELICOPTER SHOT

Dhoni is famous for his use of the "helicopter shot." This technique involves lifting the bat high into the air and then whipping the wrists to spin the bat around, generating power and elevation. While playing against Australia in 2012, Dhoni used this method to hit a six that traveled a mind-boggling 367 feet—one of the biggest shots in cricket history!

India is crowned **World Cup winner** for the first time in twenty-eight years!

TEAM USA
STUNS USSR IN OLYMPIC HOCKEY VICTORY

Heading into the Winter Olympics, the Soviet Union ice hockey team had a fifth consecutive gold medal in their sights. They expected to cruise to victory, but were stopped in their tracks by a group of young American amateurs who stunned the world with a shocking win.

In 1980, professional players were not eligible to play in the Olympics, so US head coach Herb Brooks put together a team of university students for the Games in Lake Placid, New York.

The youngsters exceeded expectations by making it through to the medal round, where they faced a Soviet Union side who ignored the rules and fielded a team full of world-class players. Those same players had crushed the USA 10–3 in a warm-up game just two weeks earlier. Brooks's boys needed to produce a miracle to beat them this time, and that is exactly what they did. They showed immense character in the semifinal to hold off the Soviet onslaught and record one of the biggest upsets in sports history.

It's a nightmare start for the US—Vladimir Krutov deflects a slapshot from Alexei Kasatonov, which glides past the goalie to give the Soviets the lead.

1ˢᵗ PERIOD		
🇺🇸	USA	0
☭	USSR	1

But US star Buzz Schneider finds space on the left wing—he moves his stick high above his head. *WHACK!* He unleashes a ferocious shot that flies into the top corner.

The USA is on the scoreboard!

1ˢᵗ PERIOD		
🇺🇸	USA	1
☭	USSR	1

1ˢᵗ PERIOD		
🇺🇸	USA	1
☭	USSR	2

There's no time to relax as the Soviets continue to attack. Sergei Makarov powers through the USA defense. He guides a delicate wrist shot home to put them back in front.

As the first period draws to a close, US forward Dave Christian tries his luck from way out. SMACK! His slapshot has power but it shouldn't trouble the world's best goalie, Vladislav Tretiak . . .

1st PERIOD		
🇺🇸	USA	2
☭	USSR	2

who makes an easy save. But what's this? Tretiak misplays the rebound, the puck falls straight to Mark Johnson, who equalizes with one second on the clock!

Soviet coach Viktor Tikhonov replaces Tretiak after his costly error. The team responds well as Aleksandr Malstev breaks away and restores the USSR's lead.

The USA gets another chance at a goal after a wild effort from Dave Silk falls Mark Johnson's way. He makes no mistake, sliding the puck through the legs of the goalie.

2ND PERIOD		
🇺🇸	USA	2
☭	USSR	3

It's neck and neck!

3rd PERIOD		
🇺🇸	USA	3
☭	USSR	3

The Soviets look shell-shocked. They can't reach US captain Mike Eruzione as he shifts the puck to his left and . . .

WHOOSH!

3RD PERIOD		
🇺🇸	USA	4
☭	USSR	3

launches a low wrist shot that slams into the net. The USA pulls ahead for the first time. Can they hold on?

They can!

The young Americans have beaten the mighty Soviets. Commentator Al Michaels roars,

"Do you believe in miracles? YES!"

JESSE OWENS
JUMPS FOR GOLD

Nobody personified Olympic values more than the legendary Jesse Owens. His incredible athletic record speaks for itself—he excelled in sprinting and long jump—but he was also a huge inspiration away from the track.

t was obvious Owens was going to be the star of the 1936 Olympics Games in Berlin from the start.

The twenty-two-year-old American powered to victory in the 100-meter dash, and a day later, Owens chalked up his second gold in the long-jump after a close-fought battle with Germany's own Luz Long. The 200-meters proved far easier for Owens as he cruised to victory in Olympic-record time. To top it all off, he claimed yet another gold as part of the USA team in the 4 x 100-meter relay, where they set a new world record of 39.8 seconds. In doing so, Owens became the first American to win four golds at a single Games!

Crouching low toward the sand, Owens gets ready for his second event: the long jump.

He powers away from the starting line, and his strong sprinting gives him a fantastic start.

Hitting top speed, Owens is at full stride, and his eyes are fixed on the take-off board.

His foot touches the board just for a moment . . .

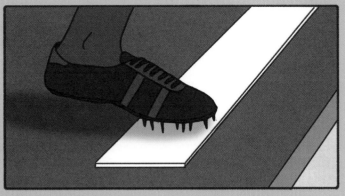

Lift off! Flying through the air, he thrusts himself forward, his arms and legs at full stretch . . .

TENSE GAMES

The 1936 Olympics were held in a tense, politically charged atmosphere. Adolf Hitler's Nazi Party had taken power in 1933, and Berlin was awarded the Games two years later. Hitler's racist policies led to international debate about a boycott of the Games; however, Owens was determined to compete and became the most successful athlete at the event. As a Black man, he was credited with single-handedly crushing Hitler's myth of white supremacy.

before crashing down feet-first into the sandpit . . .

and throwing himself forward onto his hands and knees.

The jump is measured at an incredible **26.4 feet**—more than enough for a delighted Owens to take **gold!**

KAORI ICHO

MAKES OLYMPIC WRESTLING HISTORY

To win a medal of any color at an Olympic Games is a monumental achievement—something most athletes can only dream of. To strike gold at four separate Games is almost impossible. But nothing is out of the question for the incredible wrestler Kaori Icho.

Japanese star Icho had won every Olympic match she had ever been in by the time she arrived at the 2016 Games in Rio, Brazil.

But when she faced Russia's Valeria Koblova in the 58 kilograms women's freestyle final bout, she was staring a rare defeat in the face. Trailing 2–1 with the clock ticking down, Icho reminded everyone why she's the best women's wrestler in history. Usually the attacker, Icho found herself having to counter Koblova's attempt to secure a leg hold. Proving to the world she was the ultimate all-rounder, Icho responded superbly by applying a takedown of her own. With just six seconds to go, she managed to hold on to her opponent, the referee flashed up two points, and victory was hers—along with a slice of Olympic history!

Icho and Koblova stare each other down like warriors ready for battle.

PEEP!

The two wrestlers grapple as the action begins.

PEEP!

The whistle rings out again as Koblova is penalized for being too passive. Icho scores the first point.

2-1

The Russian responds with a single leg grab to take the lead.

Icho fights back. She takes her opponent down to the floor!

Koblova holds firm, the referee calls a stalemate and orders the pair back to their feet.

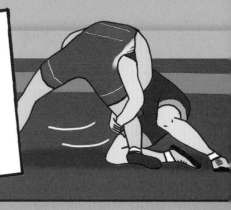

With only thirty seconds to go, Icho goes on the attack—but Koblova counters and has her leg in her grasp.

Icho counters with a takedown and flips her opponent over!

There's less than ten seconds to go, and Icho just needs to hold on . . .

TAKEDOWN

Icho secured her victory with a takedown that demonstrated all of her skill. Takedowns are worth anything between two and five points, with maximum points offered to those that are most impressive. Rather than going for the higher-scoring takedowns, Icho took Koblova onto her side, holding on with complete control to secure the two points she needed for the win!

and she does, with all her might!

3-2

An Olympic hero in every sense, Icho is all smiles as she picks up an incredible

fourth gold medal.

It's glory for Icho again!

MARIELLE GOITSCHEL
SIGNS OFF WITH SLALOM GOLD

Marielle Goitschel was the undisputed queen of the slopes throughout the 1960s. The French alpine skier won countless gold medals, including one on her final slalom run at the 1968 Olympic Games in her home country.

Four years earlier, at the Innsbruck Winter Games in Austria, eighteen-year-old Marielle won silver in the Olympic slalom, while her older sister Christine won the gold.

Two days later, Marielle won gold in the giant slalom, while Christine tied for the silver. Marielle returned to the Olympic Games in 1968 in Grenoble, France, and won another gold medal, this time in the slalom race. Flying down the mountain, weaving through the gates, Marielle's first run came in at a lightning-quick 40.27 seconds. A decent time was all she needed from her second, and she clocked an impressive 45.59 seconds to take home the top prize a massive twenty-nine seconds in front of second place! She retired that year, but her total of five Olympic medals, including three golds, plus eleven World Championship medals, makes her one of the most successful female skiers of all time.

Standing at the top of the slope at the start of her second run, Goitschel winks to the crowd.

She plants her ski poles into the snow, leans forward, and thrusts herself onto the course.

Coming through the first gate, Goitschel stares down the slope and assesses her line. It's looking good!

Crouching down to navigate the tight turns, she begins to pick up some serious speed . . .

SWOOSH!

TOP THWACK

Slalom is one of the most powerful and technical events in skiing. It involves speed, strong turns, rhythm, and confidence as the skier skis downhill and negotiates a series of gates or poles that are set out around the course. Skiiers travel through the gates in slalom, rather than around them. This is where you hear the "thwack, thwack" of plastic on plastic as the skier "clears" or "blocks" the gate as they pass.

Approaching a series of quick gates . . .

Goitschel travels through the first and THWACK! She hits the poles . . .

Her body stays true to the line as she guides her way through with her arms as THWACK! Goitschel clears another gate.

THWACK! Goitschel smashes the final gate, her arms working in rhythm with her body.

Crouching down again, she sets her sights on the finish . . .

ARRIVÉE

Goitschel digs her poles into the ground for one last push and powers over the line. Victory is hers!

LEWIS HAMILTON'S
FIRST WORLD TITLE

Winning the Formula One World title is something only the very best drivers have achieved. The legendary Lewis Hamilton has won it seven times. His first world title was earned in epic style on one of the final corners of the final race of the 2008 season.

At the final Grand Prix of the 2008 season at Interlagos in Brazil, things were quite clear for British racing driver Hamilton: finish fifth and the world title was his.

It seemed a simple task for the McLaren star who had been winning races all year. But when he found himself in sixth place on the final lap, he was staring disappointment in the face. Up ahead, Brazilian title rival Felipe Massa was greeted by the checkered flag and his Ferrari team went wild as the crown was in their grasp. But their celebrations were cut short. Approaching the final bend, Hamilton sensed an opportunity. With others ahead of him struggling in the wet conditions, the Brit swept past, surged up the hill, and flew over the finish line to finish fifth and beat Massa to the championship by a single point in the most dramatic finale to a Formula One campaign.

Just three laps to go and disaster strikes for Hamilton as he's overtaken by German Sebastian Vettel and drops down to sixth.

Vettel pulls away from Hamilton, who is going to need a miracle now.

Meanwhile, title rival Massa crosses the line to win the race. Massa's Ferrari team are going wild in the paddock—they think the title is in the bag!

But Hamilton isn't giving up without a fight. With his eyes fixed forward and gloves gripping the wheel, he picks up the pace.

But wait, here comes Hamilton! Approaching one of the final bends, he goes for one last shot at glory.

ZOOM!

He sweeps up the inside of Timo Glock, who is struggling to keep pace on such a wet track.

Hamilton completes the pass and surges back into fifth place.

Not far from the finish line now, Hamilton just needs to keep his car on the road.

He's done it! Hamilton speeds over the line as one of the most incredible races of all time comes to a close.

Hamilton points to the sky in celebration and a
Formula One legend is born.

NEED FOR SPEED

Hamilton completed the Brazilian Grand Prix in just under one and a half hours. With a total race distance of 190 miles, his average speed was clocked at an incredible 120 miles per hour, about the same speed at which a tornado spins!

KELLY CLARK

LANDS A 1080

The world's greatest sportspeople don't just win medals or trophies. They push boundaries, inspire others, and take their sports to levels that have never been seen before. By pulling off a 1080 in a competition, Kelly Clark, the snowboarding pioneer, did just that.

Standing at the top of the Superpipe at the 2011 Winter X Games in Aspen, Colorado, Clark knew she had already secured the gold medal.

Her final run was about more than that. It was a victory lap—one that would forever write her name into the history books. After dropping in, the American sped up the pipe's enormous wall and appeared to fly into the Colorado sky. Spinning, twisting, turning, Clark glided through the air like a merry-go-round that had come loose. And when she came back to earth, she touched down flawlessly to land a trick that no woman before her had managed.

Clark has the gold medal in the bag as she eyes a piece of history with her final run.

Here she goes! Clark drops in with the gleaming superpipe in front of her.

Approaching the enormous wall, the American is about to take off.

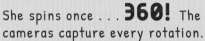

She spins once . . . **360!** The cameras capture every rotation.

Clark launches herself into the night sky.

Twice . . . **720!** Clark is so high now, the crowd has to arch their necks just to catch a glimpse of her!

Three times . . . **1080!** The crowd is willing her to land safely.

THWACK! Her board thumps the snow.

SPIN IT TO WIN IT

To pull off a 1080 trick, a snowboarder must rotate 1080 degrees in the air. That's three full turns. A rider normally tries to get at least six feet in the air to give them enough time to spin before hitting the ground. Clark's highest point was measured at nearly ten feet, and by getting so high, she was able to rotate slower. That allowed her to not just pull off the trick, but to do it with style. And, after all, style is what snowboarding is all about!

The crowd roars—Clark has pulled off a
historic 1080!

GERMANY
SHATTERS BRAZIL'S WORLD CUP DREAMS

The Brazilian national soccer team rarely loses matches. And losing on home soil is almost unheard of. Even when the mighty Germany came to town for the semifinal of the 2014 World Cup, nobody could have predicted what they were about to witness.

On a scorching summer night at the Estádio Mineirão in Belo Horizonte, Brazil, the Germans produced a red-hot performance that was among the greatest in World Cup history.

With Brazil missing talisman Neymar as a result of injury, the visitors went on the attack with ruthless ease. In nineteen wild first-half minutes, Germany plundered five goals to end the match before it had even started, and then grabbed a sixth and a seventh in the second half to leave the home crowd in tears. As the final whistle blew, the shell-shocked Brazilian players fell to their knees. The Germans advanced to a record eighth World Cup final and would go on to beat Argentina to prove themselves the best team on the planet.

It doesn't get much bigger than this. The World Cup semifinal: Brazil versus Germany. Two giants of soccer preparing for battle.

The referee's whistle goes and the tournament's most anticipated game is under way.

Eleven minutes in and Germany's Toni Kroos swings in a corner toward the six-yard box . . .

11:00

and, completely unmarked, forward Thomas Müller steers home a volley.

GOAL!

Brazil   0
Germany   1

Next, German striker Miroslav Klose takes aim from close range. The first effort is saved, but he pounces on the rebound and . . .

GOAL!

23:00

Brazil	0
Germany	2

Germany's Miroslav Klose put Germany up 2–0 with a typical poacher's finish. The goal was his sixteenth at the World Cup, and with it, he overtook Brazil legend and record-breaker Ronaldo to become the competition's all-time leading goal scorer.

Only one minute has passed and it gets worse for the hosts as Kroos smashes an epic drive into the bottom corner!

24:00

Brazil	0
Germany	3

Brazil is all over the place as Germany carves them open again just minutes later . . .

26:00

and Kroos helps himself to his second goal of the night with an easy tap-in.

Brazil	0
Germany	4

It's getting embarrassing now as defensive midfielder Sami Khedira gets in on the action as an unlikely scorer . . .

29:00

Brazil	0
Germany	5

69:00

Brazil	0
Germany	6

Finally the Brazilian defense toughens up, but after forty minutes, Germany hit back strong with André Schürrle scoring.

79:00

Brazil	0
Germany	7

And oh my, it's seventh heaven for the Germans as Schürrle suddenly smacks another shot—**BACK OF THE NET!**

89:00

Brazil	1
Germany	7

But Brazil isn't going down without a fight. Oscar lifts the ball over goalie Manuel Neuer. A goal for Brazil—at long last!

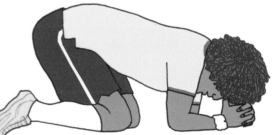

The final whistle sounds and the Brazilian players collapse to the ground.

What an epic upset!

TOMMIE SMITH AND JOHN CARLOS

BRING RACIAL INJUSTICE CENTER STAGE

The Olympics are enjoyed by viewers around the globe. So when American sprinters Tommie Smith and John Carlos took to the medal stand at the 1968 Games in Mexico City, they brought racial injustice to the attention of the entire world.

The 16th of October 1968 is a momentous day in sporting history.

Months before, members of the USA track team had threatened to boycott the Olympic Games to protest racism and to promote better conditions for Black athletes. As key organizers in the Olympic Project for Human Rights, Smith and Carlos were at the forefront of the possible boycott that caused a media frenzy. In the end, it did not take place, and so the pair used the Games to highlight racial injustice on the world stage. Smith powered to victory in the 200-meters in world-record time, with Carlos not far behind in third. On the medal stand, the American national anthem began to play. They bowed their heads and raised black-gloved fists into the air. Together they symbolized strength in the face of injustice.

As the starting pistol rings out across the stadium, Smith pushes out of lane three, and Carlos erupts out of the blocks in lane four.

The sprinters approach the first bend—Smith begins to struggle and Carlos takes an early lead.

But Smith appears to find a burst of speed on the straight and powers through.

Carlos glances to his left and **WHOOSH!**

Smith surges past him into the lead!

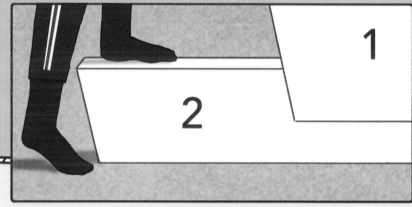

Smith crosses the line to win gold in a world-record time of 19.83 seconds, while Carlos takes bronze.

As Smith and Carlos walk to the podium to receive their medals, they display black socks to the watching world.

A POWERFUL MESSAGE

Smith and Carlos donned black socks with no shoes to represent Black poverty, while Smith wore a black scarf around his neck, standing for Black pride. Carlos also wore beads for those who died due to slavery and raised his left fist to represent Black unity; Smith raised his right fist in a Black Power salute. Their actions were seen as a controversial act, combining sports and politics.

The American National Anthem begins to play. **Carlos and Smith drop their heads and raise their black-gloved fists.**

It's an iconic moment in the history of sports that will be remembered for the rest of time.

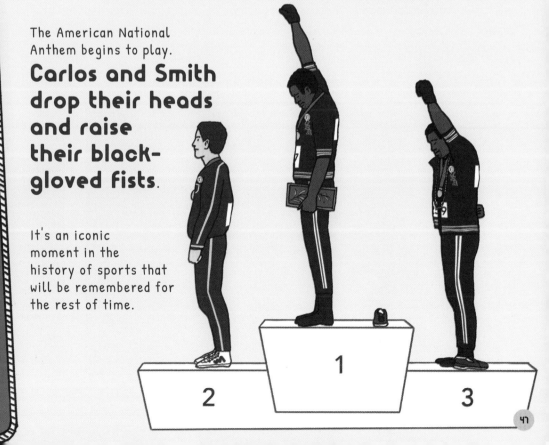

MA LONG'S
THIRD TIME ON TOP OF THE WORLD

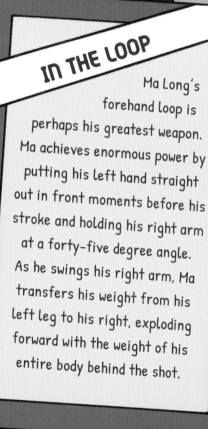

The longest-serving world number one in table tennis history, Ma Long reigned supreme in the sport for a record thirty-four months from 2015-18. And when he won his third world title in 2019, he proved himself to be one the greatest male players to ever pick up a paddle.

Ma was untouchable at the 2019 World Championships in Budapest, Hungary.

The Chinese legend—nicknamed "The Dragon"—breezed through the early rounds and into the final, where he met Sweden's Matias Falck. After Ma raced into a 2–0 lead, Falck hit back to take game three, but Ma claimed the next game and then battled his way to match point in the fifth. As Ma tossed the ball up for one final serve, Falck nudged a forehand return over the net, but it was quickly on its way back at super speed. With no time to react, Falck hit the net on his return and Ma secured a 4–1 victory. He dropped his paddle on the floor, raised both arms to the crowd, and let out a huge roar—a third world crown title was his!

IN THE LOOP

Ma Long's forehand loop is perhaps his greatest weapon. Ma achieves enormous power by putting his left hand straight out in front moments before his stroke and holding his right arm at a forty-five degree angle. As he swings his right arm, Ma transfers his weight from his left leg to his right, exploding forward with the weight of his entire body behind the shot.

It's match point and Ma prepares to serve. He holds his paddle tightly in his right hand, the ball in his left.

As he tosses the ball high into the air, his eyes do not blink.

The ball drops toward the table. **PING!**

Ma caresses the ball with a delicate forehand.

It bounces to his left before spinning to the center of Falck's side of the table.

The Swede is onto it quickly. Falck lunges forward . . .

PONG! His paddle connects with a forehand swing.

Falck attempts to give Ma a taste of his own medicine with a smashed return. It's a great effort as the ball lands to the right of Ma—who is at full stretch! But Ma pulls his arm back.

He lashes it forward . . .

SMACK!

to unleash his deadly forehand loop, which has Falck scrambling!

A deafening cry echoes around the stadium . . .

And Falck's return only goes and crashes into the net!

Ma is a three-time world champion!

JONNIE PEACOCK

BREAKS PARALYMPIC 100-METER T44 RECORD

Before the 2012 Paralympic Games, the name Jonnie Peacock would not have meant much to most people. But the amputee sprinter became a household name after an incredible eleven seconds in which he delivered one of the most electrifying performances in the history of the Games.

"Pea-cock, Pea-cock, Pea-cock," screamed eighty thousand fans at London's Olympic Stadium.

They could sense something special was about to happen as their homegrown hero took his marks at the start of the T44 100-meter final. Despite being the world record holder, Peacock was only nineteen years old, and was up against a field of more established world-class sprinters. As he flew out of the blocks, the fans's roar grew louder. Neck and neck with America's Richard Browne until the final 30 meters, the Brit pulled away, and as he approached the 100-meter mark, he took a quick look behind him. Nobody in sight—victory was his! A smile beamed across his face as he crossed the line in a Paralympic record of 10.90 seconds. Peacock had won gold, as well as the hearts of an entire nation.

Peacock gives his fans a big smile as his name is chanted around the stadium before the race.

The sprinter takes his marks and arches his back toward the sky.

BLADE TO MEASURE

At just five years old, Peacock contracted meningitis and had his right leg amputated below the knee. As a result, he runs with a blade that is made from carbon fiber and designed to mimic human tendons and muscles. It does so by storing energy as the blade bears Peacock's weight before releasing that energy when he pushes off the ground.

Peacock's out of the blocks as soon as the starting gun blasts. It's the perfect start!

He's ahead—just! But Browne is on his tail.

As the pack reaches the 30-meter mark, Peacock and Browne begin to pull away.

Peacock hits top speed—ZOOM!

Peacock's absolutely flying now and is starting to put some distance between himself and Browne.

As he approaches the finish line, Peacock takes one look to his left to check who is there . . .

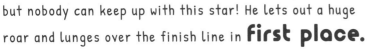

but nobody can keep up with this star! He lets out a huge roar and lunges over the finish line in **first place.**

And in **paralympic-record time** as well! A delighted Peacock shows off his gold medal to the adoring London crowd.

SUPER SKILLS

There are a certain set of skills that super-elite athletes possess that allow them to reach to the highest levels of sport, ranging from anatomical and physiological, to enviable traits and strong, admirable characteristics. The sportspeople featured in this book are some of the best athletes in the world, and their incredible abilities are truly a sight to behold.

The statistics featured in this section are correct at time of print.

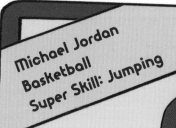

Michael Jordan
Basketball
Super Skill: Jumping

Earning the nickname "His Airness," Michael Jordan was the absolute master of the slam dunk. His incredible offense, determination, and all-round skill propelled him to the NBA scoring title ten times. Arguably the greatest basketball player ever, Jordan led the Chicago Bulls to six NBA championships.

Height
6'6"

Max vertical jump
47.6 inches

NBA All-Star appearances
14

NBA points
32,292

Three-pointers
581

Bethany Hamilton
Surfing
Super Skill: Physical strength

After losing her arm as a child, Bethany Hamilton had to adapt on the waves. Surfing requires endurance, a strong core, and upper-body strength, and as a result, Hamilton has developed tremendous strength as she paddles twice as hard and is forced to kick with her feet to compensate.

Height
5'11"

Highest wave surfed
39 feet

Heats surfed
22

Competition wins
7

ESPY awards
1

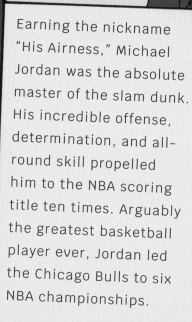

Muhammad Ali
Boxing
Super Skill: Speed

Considered by many as the best athlete of all time, there was so much to admire about the legendary Muhammad Ali. But it was his incredible lightning speed that set him apart from the rest. He practiced his speed by dodging rocks thrown at him by his younger brother, Rudy.

Height
6'3"

Arm reach
6.5 feet

Bouts
61

Wins
56

World title defenses
19

Usain Bolt
Track and field
Super Skill: Stride length

Nobody has dominated sprinting quite like Usain Bolt, thanks largely to his enormous stride length. Most elite sprinters take around 45 strides to complete a 100-meter race, but Bolt's long legs mean he typically finishes in around 41 strides— Incredible!

Height
6'5"

Stride length
8.1 feet

100m PB
9.58 seconds

200m PB
19.19 seconds

Top speed
27.78 mph

Jayne Torvill
Ice skating
Super Skill: Elegance

There is nothing quite like watching Jayne Torvill glide around the ice. She managed to remain elegant while hitting speeds that would make most people's heads spin. With partner Christopher Dean, she revolutionized ice dancing to become one of the most revered dancers in the sport.

Height
5'3"

Olympic golds
1

World Champ golds
4

European Champ golds
4

British figure skating golds
7

Christopher Dean
Ice skating
Super Skill: Choreography

Before the emergence of Christopher Dean and his partner Jayne Torvill, ice dancers would perform routines that used several pieces of music. But Dean choreographed routines using one piece of music that would tell dramatic stories much like the emotional performances viewers would expect to see in the theater.

Height
5'11"

Olympic golds
1

World Champ golds
4

European Champ golds
4

Routines choreographed
113

Michael Phelps
Swimming
Super Skill: Double joints

Michael Phelps was born to swim. His double-jointed ankles bent 15 percent more than other swimmers and his huge feet meant his legs acted almost like flippers in the water. Couple that with a steely determination and it is no wonder he finished his career as the most decorated Olympian of all time!

Height
6'4"

Shoe size
14

Best event
Butterfly

Armspan
6.6 feet

Olympic golds
23

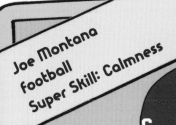

Dwight Clark
Football
Super Skill: Determination

Dwight Clark will forever be remembered for his part in "The Catch" when he combined with team-mate Joe Montana in 1981. But Clark had an excellent career in his own right. Averaging sixty-six catches per season between 1980 and 1986, Clark was one of the most determined players to pick up a football.

Height
6'4"

NFL appearances
134

Receiving touchdowns
48

Receiving yards
6,750

Super Bowl wins
2

Joe Montana
Football
Super Skill: Calmness

American football icon Joe Montana seemed to have the ability to slow the game down in front of him. The quarterback known as "Joe Cool" remained calm in the most pressured situations, leading the San Francisco 49ers to NFL domination in the 1980s.

Height
6'2"

NFL appearances
192

Passing touchdowns
273

Super Bowl wins
4

Super Bowl MVPs
3

Billie Jean King
Tennis
Super Skill: Power

Given the power she put into her strokes on the court, it is amazing that Billie Jean King had any energy left to fight for parity. But that is exactly what she did. While campaigning for equal pay for women in tennis, King powered her way to 129 career titles with her hard-hitting shots.

Height
5'5"

Played
Right-handed

Grand Slam singles titles
12

Grand Slam doubles titles
27

Career win rate
82 percent

Tiger Woods
Golf
Super Skill: Perfect swing

It was his perfect swing that propelled Tiger Woods to golfing greatness. His club reached speeds of more than 125 miles per hour, and he has a knack for keeping his arms perfectly in line as he drives from the tee, creating incredible power.

Height
6'1"

Top club speed
129.2 mph

Longest drive
498 yards

PGA tour wins
82

Majors wins
15

Anna van der Breggen
Cycling
Super Skill: Endurance

One of cycling's greatest all-rounders, Anna van der Breggen excels on the climbs. Possessing enormous leg power and incredible endurance, she is able to accelerate away from her rivals on the uphill and maintain her speed no matter how brutal the climb.

Height
5'6"

Specialist event
Time trials

Pro career wins
62

Olympic golds
1

World Champ golds
3

Jackie Robinson
Baseball
Super Skill: Base stealing

A baseball trailblazer, Jackie Robinson is one of sport's most inspiring figures. His impact off the field will never be forgotten, nor will his exploits on it. He was a bold player, often stealing bases, and he famously stole home for the Brooklyn Dodgers against the New York Yankees in 1955.

Height
5'11"

Hits
1,563

Home runs
141

Runs batted in
761

Stolen bases
200

Cathy Freeman
Track and field
Super Skill: Mental strength

When Cathy Freeman won gold at the Sydney Olympics in 2000, she did much more than run 400 meters faster than any other woman. In crossing the finish line first, Freeman overcame the expectations of twenty million sports-mad Australians and became an icon of mental strength and resilience.

Height
5'5"

400m PB
48.63 seconds

Olympic golds
1

World Champ golds
2

Commonwealth Games golds
4

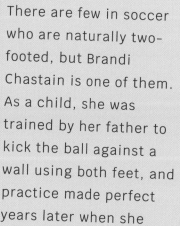

Brandi Chastain
Soccer
Super Skill: Two-footed

There are few in soccer who are naturally two-footed, but Brandi Chastain is one of them. As a child, she was trained by her father to kick the ball against a wall using both feet, and practice made perfect years later when she scored a left-footed penalty that won the 1999 World Cup for USA.

Height
5'7"

USA caps
192

USA goals
30

World Cup wins
2

Olympic golds
2

Simone Biles
Gymnastics
Super Skill: Dedication

Beginning her elite career in 2011, Simone Biles took gymnastics by storm and is already thought to be the sport's greatest ever competitor. Biles became known for her gravity-defying floor routines, and even though her skills are ahead of her competition, she still is dedicated to adding new elements to every routine.

Height
4'8"

Take-off speed
14.7 mph

Highest jump (floor routine)
9.6 feet

Olympic golds
4

World Champ golds
19

M.S. Dhoni
Cricket
Super Skill: Power hitting

With huge forearms and spectacular strength, M.S. Dhoni packed a punch with almost every strike of a cricket ball. A specialist in One-Day International (ODI) cricket, the Indian legend was a key member of the Test team who saved his best shots for when his team needed him the most—like during the 2011 World Cup.

Height
5'11"

ODI matches
350

ODI runs
10,773

ODI sixes
229

Test runs
4,876

Jesse Owens
Track and field
Super Skill: Speed

Jesse Owens is one of the most famous track-and-field athletes of all time. At the 1936 Berlin Olympics, Owens's incredible speed captured gold in the 100 meters, long jump, 200 meters, and 4×100 meter relay, a feat that would not be matched until American Carl Lewis did the same at the 1984 Los Angeles Games.

Height
5'10"

100m personal best
10.3 seconds

200m personal best
20.7 seconds

Long jump
8.13 meters

Olympic golds
4

Kaori Icho
Wrestling
Super Skill: Defense

Japanese freestyle wrestler Kaori Icho never lost a bout at the Olympics and won her first gold at Athens in 2004, before repeating the feat at Beijing 2008, London 2012, and Rio 2016. The first female Olympian to win four consecutive titles in the same discipline, Icho has stayed on top largely due to her strong defense.

Height
5'5"

Weight
128 lb.

World Champ titles
10

Olympic golds
4

Asian Games golds
1

Marielle Goitschel
Alpine skiing
Super Skill: Rhythm

Epic speed, strong turns, and good rhythm make a great slalom skier, and Marielle Goitschel's rhythm was impeccable! The Frenchwoman glided through the gates on slopes around the world throughout the 1960s, winning eleven World Championship medals to become the greatest skier on the planet.

Height
5'7"

World Champ golds
7

Olympic golds
2

Age at first Olympic gold
18

World cup wins
7

Lewis Hamilton
Motor racing
Super Skill: Overtaking

You don't become Formula One's most successful driver without taking risks, and Lewis Hamilton is one of the sport's greatest risk-takers. Aggressive and ferociously quick at the wheel of an F1 car, the Brit loves nothing more than overtaking his opponents and has claimed seven world titles so far!

Height
5'8"

Race car number
44 for Mercedes

First F1 race
2007

F1 world titles
7

Top speed
225 mph

Kelly Clark
Snowboarding
Super Skill: Focus

For Kelly Clark, winning medals and competitions was not enough. Although she racked up more than most, the American was focussed on becoming a pioneer in her sport. She became the first-ever woman to pull off a 1080 in competition, and inspired a legion of female snowboarders to push the boundaries of the sport.

Height
5'4"

Olympic golds
1

X Games golds
7

World Snowboard Tour titles
5

ESPY awards
2

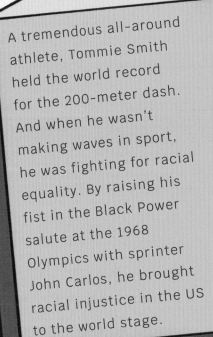

Tommie Smith
Track and field
Super Skill: Bravery

A tremendous all-around athlete, Tommie Smith held the world record for the 200-meter dash. And when he wasn't making waves in sport, he was fighting for racial equality. By raising his fist in the Black Power salute at the 1968 Olympics with sprinter John Carlos, he brought racial injustice in the US to the world stage.

Height
6'3"

200m PB
19.83 seconds

100m PB
10.10 seconds

Olympic gold medals
1

Universiade golds
1

John Carlos
Track and field
Super Skill: Courage

After winning bronze in the 200-meter dash at the 1968 Olympics, John Carlos joined teammate Tommie Smith in raising the Black Power salute. The pair were suspended by the Olympic Committee, but their courage would spark an important debate about racial injustice.

Height
6'4"

200m PB
19.92 seconds

100m PB
10.0 seconds

Olympic medal
1

Pan American Games golds
1

Ma Long
Table tennis
Super Skill: Consistency

From an early age, table tennis star Ma Long possessed a powerful forehand and worked hard to make his backhand just as impressive. As a result, "The Dragon" made himself practically unbeatable and barely lost a match in the mid–2010s. He once went on a winning streak of thirty-five sets in a row. Now that's consistency!

Height
5'9"

Olympic golds
3

World Champ golds
12

World Cup wins
7

Months as no. 1 player in world
64

Jonnie Peacock
Track and field
Super Skill: Willpower

Jonnie Peacock was only five years old when he had his right leg amputated. Fourteen years later in 2012, the British athlete made a name for himself as he was crowned Paralympic champion in front of his home crowd. By the end of June that year, he had become the world's fastest amputee sprinter!

Height
5'10"

Paralympic golds
2

World Champ golds
2

100m T44
10.64 seconds

Highest average speed
21 mph

GLOSSARY

1080 (in snowboarding) A difficult trick that involves rotating the snowboard three times.

All-around event (in gymnastics) Referring to all the events in a competition. The winner of an all-around event is the competitor with the highest combined score across all events.

Amputee A person who has had a limb amputated.

Australian Aboriginal A person who belongs or is related to one of the groups living in Australia when the Europeans arrived there.

Back handspring (in gymnastics) A tumbling move where a gymnast takes off from one or two feet, jumps backward onto their hands, and lands on their feet.

Back straight (in track and field) A straight part of a circuit farthest from the finishing point.

Backhand (in tennis) A stroke played with the back of the hand facing in the direction of the stroke, with the arm across the body.

Backstroke (in swimming) A stroke that swimmers do on their backs, kicking their legs and alternating their arms through the water.

Black Power A social, economic, and political movement of Black people to obtain self-determination.

Blade A prosthetic lower limb designed for athletes, consisting of a flattened length of carbon fiber with a long, curved section at the base.

Block (in track and field) A device used by sprint athletes to brace their feet against at the start of a race so they don't slip.

Boycott To refuse to be involved with something as a way of expressing disapproval.

Breaststroke (in swimming) A stroke that a swimmer does on their front, moving their arms and legs horizontally in a circular motion.

Bunt (in baseball) A hit in which the batter deliberately connects with the ball softly to make it more difficult to field.

Butterfly (in swimming) A stroke that swimmers do on their fronts, kicking their legs and bringing their arms over their head together.

Chip (in golf) A short approach shot that lofts the ball toward the green.

Counter (in wrestling) A move used by a wrestler to block or stop their opponent from attacking them.

Crease (in cricket) A line on the playing surface where the batter stands.

Defender A player whose role is to protect their own side's goal.

Defensive line (in football) The group of defensive players positioned on the line of scrimmage, directly opposite the offensive line.

Dribble (in basketball) When a player travels while bouncing the ball on the floor.

Duck diving A surfing technique where surfers sink their boards below the water so they can dive underneath the waves.

End zone (in football) The area at each end of the field into which the ball must be carried or passed and caught to score a touchdown.

Forehand (in tennis) A stroke played with the palm of the hand facing in the direction of the stroke.

Forehand drive (in table tennis) A basic offensive strike to force opponents into an error.

Forehand loop (in table tennis) An advanced version of the forehand drive that adds more speed, spin, and power to a shot.

Forward An attacking player.

Foul line (in basketball) The line from which a player tries to shoot the ball through the basket after they have been fouled.

Freestyle (in swimming) A competition or race in which swimmers may use a stroke of their choice instead of a specified stroke.

Freestyle (in wrestling) An event in which a wrestler can use any style or method they like.

Gates (in Alpine skiing) Two poles with colored flags on top that slalom skiers must pass through.

Goalkeeper A player whose role is to stop the ball from entering the goal.

Green (in golf) The smooth area of the course where the hole is located.

Hang time The amount of time a person can remain in the air.

Heavyweight A boxer weighing 200 pounds or more and therefore in the heaviest weight class.

Helicopter shot (in cricket) A shot that generates huge amounts of power by lifting the bat high in the air and flicking it with the wrists.

Knockout (in boxing) A situation in which a boxer wins the fight by making their opponent fall to the ground and be unable to stand up before the referee has counted to ten.

Line of scrimmage (in football) The imaginary line separating the teams at the beginning of each play.

Long jump An athletics contest that involves jumping as far as you can from a marker that you run up to.

Midfielder A player in the central part of the field.

Nazi Party A far-right political party in Germany active between 1920 and 1945.

Offensive line (in football) The group of offensive players positioned on the line of scrimmage, directly opposite the defensive line.

Olympic Project for Human Rights A former American organization that protested against racial segregation in the United States and elsewhere, and racism in sports in general.

Overhead (in tennis) A shot that involves tossing the ball into the air and hitting the ball when it is above the head.

Paddle (in table tennis) A short-handled racket.

Paddock (in motor racing) An enclosed area behind the pits where the technical staff, equipment, catering, media, and officials are located.

Peloton The main field of cyclists in a road race.

Penalty (in soccer) An opportunity to score a goal, which is given to the attacking team if the defending team breaks a rule near their own goal.

Penalty shoot-out (in soccer) A way of deciding the result of a game that has ended in a draw. Players from each team try to score a goal in turn until one player fails to score and their team loses the game.

Pitcher (in baseball) The player who delivers the ball to the batter.

Puck (in ice hockey) The small rubber disc that is used instead of a ball.

Relay (in track and field) A race in which members of a team take turns to complete different sections.

Rough (in golf) Part of the course where the grass is allowed to grow longer, making it more difficult to play from.

Round-off (in gymnastics) A tumbling skill like a cartwheel, but with both feet landing at the same time.

Run (in cricket) A score of one that is made by players running between marked areas on the pitch.

Runners (in baseball) Players from the batting team who are on the bases while the pitch is thrown and try to advance.

Sack (in football) When the quarterback is tackled behind the line of scrimmage before he can throw a forward pass.

Serve (in tennis and table tennis) The act of hitting the ball to start play.

Six (in cricket) A shot that scores six runs by hitting the ball over the boundary without hitting the ground along the way.

Slam dunk (in basketball) A shot in which a player jumps up and forces the ball down through the basket.

Slapshot (in ice hockey) A hard shot made by raising the stick about waist-high before striking the puck with a sharp slapping motion.

Snap (in football) The action in which the ball is tossed between the legs by the center. When the snap occurs, the ball is officially in play and action begins.

Soviet Union A country, made up of fifteen republics in eastern Europe and northern Asia, which no longer exists.

Straight sets A situation in which the winner of a tennis match does not lose a set.

Superpipe (in snowboarding) A large snow-covered sloping channel with a U-shaped cross section, on which snowboarders perform aerial maneuvers.

T44 A sport classification applying to athletes who have had one leg amputated below the knee.

Takedown (in wrestling) A term used to describe bringing an opponent to the floor.

Time trial (in cycling) A contest in which competitors race along a course individually, in as fast a time as possible, instead of racing directly against one another.

Touchdown (in football) A six-point score made by carrying or passing the ball into the end zone of the opposing side.

Volley (in tennis) An act of hitting the ball before it touches the ground.

White supremacy A form of racism, it is the belief that white people are superior to people from all other racial and ethnic groups.

Wicket (in cricket) A set of three upright sticks with two small sticks on top of them at which the ball is bowled. There are two wickets on a cricket pitch.

Wrist shot (in ice hockey) A type of shot in which the puck is swept along the ice against the stick and then released with a rotating motion of the wrists.